COME DOWN, LORD!

COME DOWN, LORD!

Roger Ellsworth

THE BANNER OF TRUTH TRUST

THE BANNER OF TRUTH TRUST
3 Murrayfield Road, Edinburgh EH12 6EL, UK
P.O. Box 621, Carlisle, PA 17013, USA

*

© Roger Ellsworth 1988
First published 1988
Revised edition 2009
Reprinted 2012
Reprinted 2018

ISBN: 978 1 84871 039 9

*

Typeset in 10.5/15 pt Sabon Oldstyle at
The Banner of Truth Trust, Edinburgh

Printed in the USA by
Versa Press, Inc.
East Peoria, IL

TO SYLVIA

CONTENTS

I

WE MISS YOU

Look down from heaven, and behold from the habitation of thy holiness and of thy glory: where is thy zeal and thy strength, the sounding of thy bowels and of thy mercies toward me? are they restrained?

Doubtless thou art our father, though Abraham be ignorant of us, and Israel acknowledge us not; thou, O LORD, art our father, our redeemer: thy name is from everlasting. (Isaiah 63:15-16)

Isaiah was given a preview of his people's future. He could see the Babylonians coming in, ravaging the land, taking the people into captivity, and leaving their homeland utterly desolate and barren. He could see the people languishing in captivity and yearning for their home as year after dreary year passed away. Finally, he could see the people restored to their land, and he could see that restoration as a symbol of the coming Messiah who would establish an everlasting kingdom.

The passage we shall be studying is a prayer the prophet prayed as he visualized his people at their very lowest ebb. He could see them in captivity in Babylon when the situation was at its worst, and he was moved to pray the prayer that would be in their hearts and on their lips at that dreadful time.

The heart of this prayer is expressed in those poignant words: 'Come down, Lord . . . ' (64:1). Everything else seems to lead to or flow from that one petition. In the rest of the prayer we have the prophet arming himself with arguments to persuade God to return to his people in blessing and power. These are arguments we might use to persuade an estranged or offended family member to return and restore a broken relationship.

As we follow Isaiah's arguments we shall certainly see, with a smidgen of perception, how fitting they are for us to employ. We, like Israel, are far from God and we are not realizing his blessings. We are in desperate need of his renewing and reviving presence. Let us even now begin to cry with Isaiah: 'Come down, Lord!' Let us arm ourselves with the same arguments he used, and hoist our voices to heaven in such numbers and with such frequency and intensity, that God will be moved to visit us in mighty power. Let us unite our voices to make this a swelling chorus that will constantly bombard the gates of heaven. Let us resolve even now to give ourselves no rest and to give God no rest until the people of God be 'a praise in the earth' (*Isa.* 62:6-7).

The first argument Isaiah employs to persuade God to come down is in the opening words of his prayer. He seems to be saying: 'Come down, Lord, we miss you.' Have you ever missed someone? Then you know what it is to have your mind drawn to the special traits and actions of the one you miss. Perhaps you find yourself thinking of that person's smile or recalling the warmth of a single touch. Maybe you have even reproached yourself for not really enjoying and appreciating that special person's presence. If so, you should be able to feel the dull ache of Isaiah's words as he describes the things his people would miss about God.

First, he speaks of missing —

I. The Smiling Face of God

'Look down from heaven,' he says. How appropriate for him to begin here. He realizes the people could not get anything else from God until they first got him to look down and take notice of their wretched condition. He realizes that God had, in effect, turned his face away from them. He had left them to themselves. They had imagined they could manage quite nicely without God and had dashed recklessly off into sin.

This may come as a shock to many. The popular notion of God has him sitting in heaven and smiling benignly upon us no matter what we choose to do. We seem to have forgotten what Isaiah brings out about God — his habitation is one of 'holiness' and 'glory' (63:15). We have become broadminded and tolerant of sin, jesting about it and winking at it; but God remains unalterably opposed to it. We may negotiate with sin and ultimately declare détente with it, but God never will. When we begin to smile complacently upon sin, he stops smiling on us and turns his face away.

3

Does this surprise you? It should not. God long ago established this as his policy toward sin in the lives of his people. He left no doubt about this early in the history of the people of Israel. Here is how he promised to deal with their sins:

> I will forsake them, and I will hide my face from them, and they shall be devoured, and many evils and troubles shall befall them; so that they will say in that day, 'Are not these evils come upon us, because our God is not among us?' And I will surely hide my face in that day for all the evils which they shall have wrought, in that they turned unto other gods. (*Deut.* 31:17-18)

Nothing is more satisfying and thrilling than living in the consciousness of God smiling upon us, and nothing is more dreadful than living without that smile. Is this not the reason the church is as she is? She has all kinds of slick promotions, attractive programmes, and entertaining preachers, but she is not really seeing the fullness of God's blessings because he has been grieved by her sins and has turned his face away. Let us, therefore, join Henry F. Lyte in praying: 'God of mercy, God of grace, show the brightness of thy face.'

But in addition to missing the smile of God, Isaiah mentions missing—

II. The Helping Hand of God

God had shown his power time and time again on behalf of the people of Israel. In fact, before entering upon this prayer, the prophet rehearses the greatest display of God's power on behalf of Israel. It was when he miraculously opened the Red Sea and enabled them to escape from Pharoah and his army (63:12-14).

But nothing was clearer to Isaiah than this—God was withholding his power from Israel. As he contemplated the future, he could see Israel defeated, the beautiful temple a heap of rubble, the bulk of the people carried away as slaves to Babylon. One question rushed through his head: 'Where is God?' (v. 11). So when he comes to pray this prayer, he immediately asks: 'Where is thy zeal and thy strength?' He is asking why God has not shown his energy and power for them as he had done on so many previous occasions, why he was leaving Israel to her own devices.

The people of God have often heard the world tauntingly say: 'Where is thy God?' (*Psa.* 42:3, 10; 79:10; 115:2). But it is a sad thing when the people of God have to ask themselves that question. We are happy if we can answer skeptics by pointing to present indications of God's power. But what are we to do when God withholds his power from us and there are no evidences to point out?

The church, in order to maintain credibility in the world, has to have the power of God. She is involved in a great spiritual warfare, and only God's power will enable her to prevail. Human ingenuity and wisdom are simply not equal to the task. Trying to do this kind of work without the power of God is like trying to break huge granite boulders with our bare hands.

The problem is that the church is trying to subsist on her own power. She is relying on her own abilities. Human wisdom can produce many things, and the church is trying to pass these things off as the hand of God at work, but the world is not buying it. They still bombard us with the disturbing question, 'Where is thy God?' And if we will get alone and examine our hearts, we will be driven to admit that the many things we are producing are cheap and shabby substitutes for the real power of God, and we will be compelled to cry out to God: 'Where is thy zeal and thy strength?'

Finally, in opening this prayer, Isaiah mentions missing—

III. The Caring Heart of God

He asks: 'Where is . . . the sounding of thy bowels and of thy mercies toward me? Are they restrained?'

This phrase 'the sounding of thy bowels' is the typical Hebrew expression for the yearning of the heart, the compassion of the heart.

Isaiah was asking the inevitable question. If God turns his face and withholds his strength, does that mean he no longer loves his children? As Isaiah begins to reason about this, he immediately realizes that God is still their Father. Abraham and Jacob, their fathers in the flesh, would not be willing to acknowledge them, so great was their sin, but God's name is everlasting. In other words, he is consistent in his nature. Because of his unchanging character, Isaiah knew that he would forgive Israel of her sins if she would repent. That knowledge is what encouraged Isaiah to pray this prayer.

But there is a great truth here that we must not ignore. God may never stop loving us when we get into sin, but he does withhold the expressions of his love and thus makes us think he will never love us again. We may argue and convince ourselves that God does still love us, and such reasoning is well and good, but it will never replace the actual manifestations of God's love. How much better it is not to have to convince ourselves that God loves us, but to have ready at hand abundant manifestations of his love!

The opening words of Isaiah's prayer ought to remind us of what our lives should be like. We should be conscious of the smile of God, seeing the power of God, and basking in the love of God. Nothing is greater than living in this way. And we should also realize again what a terrible thing it is to lose these things. Many of us will have to admit that we have lost them, that we are living far below where we should. If this is in fact the case, let us stop and think of the greatness of the things we are missing, and let us even now begin to cry, 'Come down, Lord, we miss you!'

Questions for Discussion

1. To what period of history does the author connect Isaiah 63:15–64:12?

2. What does the cry 'Come down, Lord!' suggest to you?

3. What evidences do you see that the church is lacking God's favour and blessing?

4. What are the sins that are causing God to hide his face from his people?

5. Read Hosea 5:15. What does God promise to do in response to the sins of his people? What would his action prompt them to do?

2

WE NEED YOU

*O LORD, why hast thou made us to err from thy ways,
and hardened our hearts from thy fear? Return for thy
servants' sake, the tribes of thine inheritance. The people
of thy holiness have possessed it but a little while: our
adversaries have trodden down thy sanctuary.*

*We are thine: thou never barest rule over them; they
were not called by thy name;*

*Oh that thou wouldest rend the heavens, that thou
wouldest come down, that the mountains might flow
down at thy presence.*

*As when the melting fire burneth, the fire causeth
the waters to boil, to make thy name known to thine
adversaries, that the nations may tremble at thy presence!*
(Isaiah 63:17–64:2)

Isaiah intensifies his appeal in these verses. He began by
urging the Lord to visit his people because they missed
his smiling face, his helping hand, and his caring heart.
Here he goes beyond that. His cry in these verses is, 'We
need you.'

This portion of Isaiah's prayer, then, signals a dramatic
change in the thinking of the people of Israel, the people

9

Isaiah was representing in this prayer. They had fondly imagined they could get along quite nicely without God; that he was, in effect, expendable. But as Isaiah looks ahead, he sees them sitting amidst the wreckage of their shattered lives; and he sees them coming, at long last, to the realization that God is not optional but essential.

Let us keep in mind that these are the people of God that Isaiah is visualizing. That is the stunning thing. One would think the need for God would have to be emphasized only to those who do not know him, but this passage is proof positive that God's people can become dangerously self-sufficient. Is the church today any different from Isaiah's people? Are we really conscious of how utterly helpless and hopeless we are apart from God? Or are we relying on our own wisdom and ability in our warfare against Satan and his forces? If we are not careful we can think pushing all the right buttons will produce lasting spiritual results. We can reduce the work of the church to shrewd manœuvring with statistical probabilities and psychological jargon. We can be guilty of doing the very thing David refused to do—fight in Saul's armour. We can have polish but not power. We need to realize that God can do more in a minute with his power than we can in a lifetime with our 'strategies!' Oh, that we could see our need of God and get a hunger for him!

These verses reveal two major reasons God's people need his power.

I. For Revival (63:17–19)

Nowhere perhaps is the tendency to rely on our own strength and wisdom stronger than in this matter of seeking revival. During the past century we have been told that revival is something we can more or less create any time we choose. It is simply a matter of employing certain techniques.

Isaiah's prayer reveals the utter folly of that notion. If it were possible for God's people to revive themselves it would have been patently absurd for him to pray in this way. But his prayer indicates clearly that the condition of the people was such that only God could help.

He first confesses the hard-heartedness of the people; and, in doing so, he reveals two ways in which hard-heartedness manifests itself (v. 17). First, the hard heart becomes increasingly insensitive to God's commands and strays from them. Secondly, the hard heart is insulated from feeling any fear for God.

In other words, when our hearts get hard toward God, we get casual and careless about sin in our lives. We grow increasingly unconcerned and indifferent about God's ways. God has certain ways for us to walk in. His are the ways of joy and righteousness (64:5), but when our hearts get hard we get filled with our own ways and pay no regard to God's ways.

I once saw a bumper sticker that read: 'There's too much apathy in this country, but who cares?' That's precisely the problem when our hearts get hard. We know we are straying from God and his ways, that we are becoming increasingly apathetic, but we simply do not care.

The other manifestation of a hard heart is in not feeling any fear of God. Christians used to talk a good deal about being God-fearing, but that term makes us nervous these days. Anytime we run across some reference in Scripture to fearing God, we always hasten to point out that this does not mean we ought to be afraid of God. I am not so sure about that. I believe there is reason to be afraid of God. God has promised to chastise his children for getting into sin. This prayer of Isaiah's is on behalf of people who were to experience the bitter pangs of chastisement. They would make this prayer theirs only after their homeland was ravaged, their temple and city were reduced to rubble, and they found themselves captive in Babylon. Who would not be afraid of such a terrible experience? Only a fool! If these people had been afraid of God and his chastisement, they could have saved themselves all manner of heartache.

But look at the cause of this hard-heartedness.

Isaiah says: 'O LORD, why hast thou made us to err from thy ways, and hardened our heart from thy fear?' According to Isaiah, God had hardened their hearts! Can this be? Or is Isaiah simply blaming God for the sins of the people? Here is something we do not hear much about, but it is a reality. When we who are God's people drift into sin, God for a while gives us opportunities to repent. If these opportunities are scorned, he just lets us go by giving us over to our sins. The first form his chastisement takes is removing from us the desire to turn back to him.

The sadness of our day is right here. We have heard for years that if we do not repent of our sins, God will send judgment upon us. We may think we are getting by with sin because things do not appear to be so bad. What most of us do not realize is God's judgment has already set in. Our very apathy about spiritual things is God's judgment upon us.

You see now how futile it is to say we can have revival any time we want. Our problem is our hearts are so hard we do not want revival. Only God can remove that hardness. No amount of promoting it will avail; we must have God.

But the prophet is not through. He goes on to say the people need God because they are downtrodden (63:18–19). Their down-troddenness is apparent in two ways. First, they were completely overcome by their enemies (v. 18), and secondly, they had even reached the point where they had become like those over whom God had never ruled. This is how the newer translations render the nineteenth verse.

God's people cannot sink lower that this—overcome by pagans and even resembling the pagans who overcame them. You do not need me to tell you how fitting this picture is of us today. Our enemies seem to be triumphing over us all around. Christian teachings are ridiculed and scorned on television and in the movies. Christianity's regard for life is monstrously defied by the wholesale slaughter of the unborn. And instead of resisting these things, many Christians are scurrying around to accommodate them. Truly, we resemble the pagans who are overcoming us!

Again I say—we need God! Only God can restore us from our down-trodden condition. Only God can remove our reproach and restore us to where we ought to be.

But we not only need God for revival, we need him also

II. For the Conversion of Sinners (64:1–2)

'Make thy name known to thine adversaries,' Isaiah prays. That is what the church is concerned about. We want to see God's name revealed to those who do not know him. But I wonder if we have fully realized what a difficult task that is and how utterly dependent we are upon God for it?

Isaiah employs three metaphors to convey what is involved in God making his name known. First, he speaks of the mountains flowing down. What an appropriate symbol the mountain is for the sinner! The sinner is a whole mountain range arrayed against God. He has in his heart mountains of opposition, hardness, stubbornness, unbelief, pride, and blindness erected against the knowledge of God.

Isaiah also mentions the coldness of water. So frigid is the heart of the sinner that every spiritual influence is soon chilled and dies. Fire to melt the ice and make the water boil is his overwhelming need.

Then Isaiah also makes mention of brushwood.

This does not come out in the King James Version which simply has the phrase: 'As when the melting fire burneth . . . '. But newer translations bring out the picture of brush. For instance, the New American Standard Bible translates the opening words of verse two in this way: 'As fire kindles the brushwood . . .'. The thing we associate with brushwood is 'tangledness.' And what a tangle the sinner's heart is! It is overgrown with all kinds of brush. Jesus talked about the heart being overgrown with the thorns of 'the cares of this world, and the deceitfulness of riches' (*Matt.* 13:22). Before the sinner can be converted, the Word of God has to find good soil in which to take root. But as long as the brush is there the Word of God cannot take root; the brush has to be burned off first.

These images should reinforce for us the truth that sinners are in the most dreadful and deplorable condition imaginable and the twin truth that sinners are not easily won to the Lord. You and I can arm ourselves with all kinds of evangelistic techniques, clever arguments, and attractive advertisements of the entertaining programmes we have down at the church; but we are still no match for the hardness, the coldness, and the tangledness of the sinner's heart. We can have our dramas and seminars, we can talk brightly about how excited we are about our church and how perky we feel because we are Christians, and the sinner will either stare blankly at us or walk away chuckling.

There is only one thing that can melt the mountain, boil the water, and consume the brush of the sinner's heart and that is the fire of God! The power of God is our need! I am convinced that the church cannot truly evangelize until she gets on her knees and seeks the convicting, converting power of God!

The church, then, has two great needs. She needs revival for herself and conversion of those who do not know God. She is completely powerless to do these things herself. Let all of us who make up the church, and who long to see revival and conversions, get on our knees and pray with Isaiah: 'Come down, Lord. We need you!'

QUESTIONS FOR DISCUSSION

1. Name some things that churches often do to bring revival that really amount to trusting in their own wisdom and strength.

2. How do you define the fear of God?

3. What are some signs of hardness of heart?

4. Name some ways in which Christians today resemble the unbelievers around them.

5. What do the three metaphors in Isaiah 64:1–2 tell us about unbelievers?

6. What is necessary to convert sinners? What things are useless?

3

WE WAIT FOR YOU

When thou didst terrible things which we looked not for, thou camest down, the mountains flowed down at thy presence.

For since the beginning of the world men have not heard, nor perceived by the ear, neither hath the eye seen, O God, beside thee, what he hath prepared for him that waiteth for him. (Isaiah 64:3-4)

Two things should be indisputably clear to us by now. First, God has power. Make no mistake about that. Isaiah speaks of mountains quaking, nations trembling, and fire raging (v. 1-2). Such language is singularly inappropriate if God does not have power. Truly, he is the God of 'awesome things' (v. 3).

Secondly, we need God's power. The church is absolutely incapable of sustaining herself. She cannot revitalize her own life, let alone bring sinners to know the life of God. Without God she is doomed to a bumbling, mumbling ineptness. 'All is vain unless the Spirit of the Holy One comes down, . . .' says the hymn writer. He has that right.

God's power and our need . . . sometimes it seems as if there is an uncrossable chasm between the two. And if we are not careful we can fix the blame on God. We can go about pitying ourselves, thinking it is our lot constantly to wring a few, meagre favours out of a miserly and reluctant God.

The problem, according to the Bible, is not at God's end. This same prophet tells us: '. . . the LORD longs to be gracious to you, And therefore He waits on high to have compassion on you' (*Isa.* 30:18, NASB). The Psalmist pictures it like this: 'How great is thy goodness, which thou hast stored up for those who fear thee, . . .' (*Psa.* 31:19). Verses like these prompted the great Charles Spurgeon to exclaim

> God is ready to help. He has everything in preparation before our needs begin. He has laid in supplies for all our wants. Before our prayers are presented, he has prepared his answers to them; . . .

If the problem is not with God, then who is left?

We are! If we are not enjoying God's power, it is because we are not utilizing the channel God has provided for receiving his power. What is that channel? It is right here in Isaiah's prayer. The prophet says God 'acts in behalf of the one who waits for him' (v. 4). Waiting on God, then, is the bridge between God's power and our need.

If this is indeed the case, we had better seek to determine what is involved in this business of waiting. Three basic elements constitute waiting on the Lord. The first is—

I. Expectation

A spirit of expectation consists of confidence, or trust, and eagerness. Let us think about the matter of trust. When we wait for someone, it is because we have the assurance or confidence that this individual will arrive at a certain time and place. Now it could very well be that this assurance is not well-founded and we shall be disappointed. Some people have the annoying habit of ignoring appointments.

But God is not undependable. His whole character is one of trustworthiness and faithfulness (*Lam.* 3:22-23). We shall not be disappointed if we wait for him. How do we know this is true? Because God has demonstrated his faithfulness in history. 'Thou didst come down, . . .' cries the prophet. He is thinking of the times in their history when God visited his people in mighty power and did terrible, or awesome things (*Exod.* 34:10, *Judg.* 5:4), things they did not expect.

There is the reason we can trust God to come down. He has come down before. Study the history of the church and you will find it to be true. The history of the church is filled with seasons of revival in which the Lord visited and refreshed his people. In America, for example, there have been great spiritual awakenings. During the colonial period people were profoundly stirred under the preaching of Jonathan Edwards, George Whitefield, and others. In 1858, revival fires began in New York City under the leadership of laymen like Jeremiah Lanphier. It is estimated that this awakening led to one million conversions. Since then there have been other significant visitations. I read recently a newspaper account of an awakening in Denver, in 1905, under the preaching of Wilbur Chapman. *The Denver Post* had this headline on January 20, 1905: 'Entire City Pauses For Prayer Even At The High Tide Of Business As The Soul Rises Above Sordid Thoughts.' Below that was a sub-headline: 'Remarkable Outburst of Gospel Sentiment Provoked by Revival.'

The history of the church is the history of revival in which God has demonstrated again and again his willingness to revive his people. In the light of these things, I say, we can wait trustingly on the Lord.

But expectation also carries the idea of eagerness. It is not simply a matter of believing that God will work on behalf of his people when they wait, but actually standing on tiptoes and stretching the neck to see it happen.

We have reason to be filled with eagerness.

Isaiah says the ear has not heard and the eye has not seen a God like our God. He always does the unexpected. Expecting him to come down and visit us means we are expecting him to do the unexpected. God will always far surpass our greatest dreams. Even as the child anticipates Christmas, let us eagerly look forward to what our God does when he revives his work.

But now we must turn from the confidence and eagerness of expectation to examine another aspect of waiting—

II. Singleness

I do not know about you, but when I am waiting on someone that is just about all I can think about. There is an element of concentration involved. You cannot do much of anything else when you are waiting.

This same element enters into our waiting on God. We have to leave out everything that would take away from our waiting. G. Campbell Morgan points out that in the Hebrew there is an affinity between the word 'wait' and the word 'entrench.' He suggests waiting means to entrench ourselves in God or dig ourselves into God.

This obviously does not mean that we should leave off all our natural and normal concerns. There have been times when Christians resigned their jobs and simply 'tarried' for the Lord. But it does mean that waiting upon God for revival should never be very far from our minds. When there is a lull in the day's activities our minds ought naturally to gravitate to this vital area.

I suggest that this matter of excluding distractions involves a quietness before the Lord. Consider these words from the prophet Jeremiah: 'The Lord is good to those who wait for Him, to the person who seeks Him. It is good that he waits silently for the salvation of the Lord' (*Lam.* 3:25, 26; NASB).

You see, the danger in this matter of seeking revival is to try to create it ourselves instead of waiting on the Lord to give it. Here is how that happens. We get talking about having revival and we more or less adopt a time when we expect it to occur. If we have not seen by that time any real evidence of revival, the temptation is to manufacture something we can pass off as revival. A philosophy has been making the rounds in recent years that goes like this: 'Do something even if it is wrong.' And churches have done a lot of wrong in their feverish desire to see good results.

This is all in opposition to the quietness of waiting. Quietness before God means recognizing our lack of wisdom and power and relying solely upon God. Morgan says:

> It is the strength that prevents the blundering activity which is entirely false and will make the true activity impossible when the definite command comes.

In other words, there must be a deep sense of humility if we are truly to wait upon God. So many give the impression that closeness to God means having a cocksure attitude and arrogance. How we need to hear what the Scripture says:

> For thus says the high and exalted One who lives forever, whose name is Holy, 'I dwell in a high and holy place, and also with the contrite and lowly of spirit in order to revive the spirit of the lowly and to revive the heart of the contrite.' (*Isa.* 57:15).

Who is it that God is looking to revive? Not the proud and boastful, but the one who is waiting quietly and submissively on God.

Finally, waiting on the Lord involves—

III. Patience

I mentioned having a time frame for revival. This tendency led one preacher to say: 'Judging by most of our church calendars, we want revival. But we want it on our schedule, and we want it fast!'

We have not yet learned that waiting on the Lord means patiently looking to him until he sees fit to move. There are some things that simply cannot be hurried. James reminds us of the patience of the farmer:

> Behold, the farmer waits for the precious produce of the soil, being patient about it, until it gets the early and late rains. You too be patient, strengthen your hearts, for the coming of the Lord is at hand (*James* 5:7, 8; NASB).

Our impatience in things spiritual reminds me of Abraham. You recall the promise given to him that he would have a son to be his heir. As he advanced in years, he began to think of the impossibility of fathering a son in old age. So he took matters into his own hands. He took his wife's maid, fathered a son, and named him Ishmael. But God was not pleased and Ishmael only created heartache. In God's own time, Isaac was born.

How often we have repeated Abraham's mistake. Unwilling to wait on God, we have taken matters into our own hands only to learn that our Ishmaels bring heartache. We can create Ishmaels, only God can create an Isaac. By patiently waiting on God we can receive God's best; by running ahead of God we receive only the second best. We may create some great commotion and call it revival, but only God can create revival.

Our need, then, is to wait on the Lord. We are to wait expectantly. We are to exclude all distractions. We are to be patient. Let us make the words of the psalmist our motto in these days: 'Wait for the LORD; be strong and let your heart take courage; yes, wait for the LORD' (*Psa.* 27:14; NASB).

QUESTIONS FOR DISCUSSION

1. What steps can you take to help yourself have a spirit of expectation for revival?

2. What steps can you take to 'dig in' to God?

3. How does the author define quietness before God?

4. What signs do you see that churches are impatient on the matter of revival?

4

WE WILL MEET YOU

Thou meetest him that rejoiceth and worketh right-eousness, those that remember thee in thy ways: behold, thou art wroth: for we have sinned: in those is continuance, and we shall be saved. (Isaiah 64:5)

There are all kinds of meetings. Some are warm and friendly, some are tense and hostile. Some are short and sweet, some are long and boring. Some repay rich dividends, some are a waste of time.

When we have a meeting of the good kind, we enjoy the company of others; we learn more about others as well as ourselves; we are encouraged and strengthened. Companionship, comprehension, comfort — these are the fruits of a good meeting.

Our text talks about the best kind of meeting anyone can ever have — a meeting with God himself. And what is it to meet God? It is to enjoy those same things we enjoy in any good meeting and more! It is companionship, comprehension, and comfort, in a deeply satisfying way.

We can make this matter of meeting God an additional reason in our persuading God to come down and visit us. We might seek to persuade an estranged friend or relative to return to us by promising to meet him or her somewhere. So let us make it our resolve to meet God.

If we are to meet God, we must understand that some conditions are involved, and we must determine to comply with those conditions. Isaiah makes them clear. First, he lays down—

I. The Requirement of Righteousness

Two things are involved in meeting this requirement. First, we must rejoice in righteousness; then we must practise it. Before we can do either, we must understand it. Righteousness is simply uprightness. It is conformity to the law, the mind, and the will of God.

Nothing turns people off quicker than talk of righteousness. In the first place our society makes light of the idea that there is any such thing as right or wrong. Right and wrong cannot be defined as far as our age is concerned. It is a matter of each individual deciding for himself. What is right for one might not be for another. Such is the thinking of our day.

But even if it be allowed that there is such a thing as righteousness, few people are prepared to accept the idea of rejoicing in it. Christians believe right and wrong can be defined, but how many Christians can say they truly rejoice in righteousness? Take David, for instance. Here was a man who rejoiced in righteousness. He says in Psalm 119:14: 'I have rejoiced in the way of thy testimonies, as much as in all riches.' In the same Psalm, he adds:

Therefore, I love thy commandments above gold; yea, above fine gold. Therefore, I esteem all thy precepts concerning all things to be right; and I hate every false way (verses 127-128).

Why is it that most of us have extreme difficulty in saying these same things? Why is it that such language makes us uncomfortable? Why are we reluctant to place the laws of God above the riches of the world as David did? Why are we hesitant to say that we hate 'every false way'?

The answer is we still harbour a very basic misunderstanding about God and his laws. We persist in being suspicious about God. We continue to think that God is out to spoil our fun, to deprive us of our happiness. We have never been able to accept the basic fact that God's commandments are wholesome and good. They are not designed to rob us of happiness, but to ensure us of it. You can resent God's commandments and rebel against them, and you will find the terrible consequences God wanted to spare you. Maude Royden neatly captures the truth of the matter by saying: 'You cannot break the Ten Commandments; all you can do is break yourself against them!'

If we are ever to get past our suspicion of God so we can truly rejoice in and practise righteousness, we must love the Lord. The apostle John makes this connection in his first epistle: 'For this is the love of God, that we keep his commandments, and his commandments are not grievous' (*1 John* 5:3).

27

But do not Christians already love the Lord?

Yes, but not with a perfect love. Our love can so wane that it appears we do not even love the Lord at all. Jesus' complaint to the Christians at Ephesus was they had left their first love (*Rev.* 2:5). They had a kind of love, but it was not the fervent, warm-hearted type they had at the first.

So there appears to be a progression in complying with this requirement of righteousness. Before we can practise righteousness we must rejoice in it, and before we can rejoice in it we must love the Lord who requires it. The question now is: How can we get to the point where we love the Lord the way we should? That brings us to look at Isaiah's second requirement for meeting the Lord. We can call it—

II. The Requirement of Remembrance

Isaiah says to God: 'Thou meetest . . . those that remember thee in thy ways . . .' We must first think about that word 'remember'. It suggests effort on our part. If we are to meet the Lord and enjoy his presence, it will be because we have diligently sought to do so. Alexander MacLaren writes:

There are so many things within us to draw us away, the duties and the joys, and the sorrows of life so insist upon having a place in our hearts and thoughts, that assuredly, unless by resolute effort, frequently repeated, we clear a space in this crowded and chattering market place, where we can stand and gaze on the white summits far beyond the bustling crowd, we shall never see them, though they are visible from every place. Unless you try to remember, you will certainly forget.

Did you catch those words 'resolute effort, frequently repeated'? They are the key to remembering and thus deepening your love for the Lord. That may come as somewhat of a surprise, because most of us probably do not associate remembering with effort. We think it is something that simply happens to us. We do not feel responsible for developing the memory. We excuse ourselves by simply saying: 'I have a terrible memory'.

Think again of Jesus' words to the church in Ephesus. After he charges them with having left their first love, he says: 'Remember therefore from whence thou art fallen, and repent, and do the first works . . .' (*Rev.* 2:5). Clearly, Jesus regarded memory as something they were responsible for.

Maybe it is time, in the parlance of the world, to call a spade a spade. The reason most of us are not meeting the Lord and receiving his power and guidance is we are not willing to put forward the necessary effort. I am not talking about putting forth effort to be saved. Scripture is crystal clear at that point. We are saved by grace, not by works (*Eph.* 2:8-9). I am talking rather about putting forth effort to live the Christian life. Far too many of us want to slip quietly into heaven wearing silver slippers instead of combat boots!

But we must not stop there. We must go on to notice what it is we are to remember. Isaiah says we are to remember God in his 'ways'. This is not a call merely to sit down and speculate about what God is like. These words assume we already have a knowledge of God, that God has already been at work in our lives. Every child of God has evidence of God in his past that he can go back to from time to time. If you long to meet God today and you are having difficulty finding him, go back to those times when you met him. Go back and look at your spiritual biography.

This makes me think of Jacob. He first encountered the Lord at a place called Bethel. There he learned that it was possible for him to have communion with the Lord. He saw a vision of heaven opened and a stairway descending all the way down to earth. The point was clear—heaven was open to him. He could live in communion with the Lord. He made a vow there to live for the Lord.

Years passed and Jacob got involved in a lot of sordid things. Finally, God spoke to Jacob: 'Arise, and go up to Bethel, . . . and Jacob said . . . I will make there an altar unto God . . .' (*Gen.* 35:1-3).

If you know the Lord as your Saviour, there is a Bethel in your past. Go back there in your mind. Relive that time when you first found the Lord, and let that time open up the channel between you and God. Bask in the love you felt for the Lord then until the rubbish that has accumulated in the channel breaks away.

If you are not really walking with God, it is not because he has moved. He is still walking where he always has—in the paths of righteousness. You can go to him today by rejoicing in and practising righteousness, and by reflecting on the sweetness of communion with him in the past. Reflect on these solemn words:

The LORD is with you, while ye be with him; and if ye seek him, he will be found of you; but if ye forsake him, he will forsake you (2 *Chron.* 15:2).

QUESTIONS FOR DISCUSSION

1. How does the author define righteousness?

2. Why do we have difficulty rejoicing in righteousness?

3. What is necessary to remember the ways of the Lord?

4. What does the author say about silver slippers and combat boots?

5

WE HAVE WRONGED YOU

Thou meetest him that rejoiceth and worketh right-eousness, those that remember thee in thy ways: behold, thou art wroth; for we have sinned: in those is continuance, and we shall be saved.

But we are all as an unclean thing, and all our right-eousnesses are as filthy rags; and we all do fade as a leaf: and our iniquities, like the wind, have taken us away.

And there is none that calleth upon thy name, that stirreth up himself to take hold of thee: for thou hast hid thy face from us, and hast consumed us, because of our iniquities. (Isaiah 64:5-7)

Here we get down to the essentials. Isaiah has been arming himself with arguments to persuade God to come down and visit his people. But why is it that God has withdrawn from his people and hidden his face? In this part of his prayer Isaiah comes to grips with that question. Nothing was to be gained by dancing around the issue, so Isaiah bluntly says: 'We have sinned' (v. 5). A little later he adds: 'Thou hast hid thy face from us, . . . because of our iniquities' (v. 7).

We have talked about missing God and needing God. We have looked at the need to wait upon God and even to go out to meet him. Now we must realize that all of these things hinge upon us addressing the sins in our lives. This is the pivotal matter. We might as well stop talking about revival if we do not intend to face up to our sins and turn from them.

In ancient times, when a king decided to visit his people, he would send a messenger ahead to announce his coming. The people would prepare for his arrival by building a 'highway'. They would fill the valleys, level out the high places, straighten out the crooked places, and remove the stones and roots from the rough places. When the highway was ready, the king would come.

The Lord wants to come and visit us. He wants to fill our lives and our churches with his glorious presence. But we must prepare the way. Each one of his people has work to do. Each one of us has a valley of sinful involvement that needs to be filled in. Each one has a high place of pride to be brought low. Each one has a crooked place where our lives have deviated from his will. Each one has an accumulation of the stones and roots of lust, envy, resentment and greed to be removed. There is work to be done!

> Prepare ye the way of the Lord, make straight in the desert a highway for our God . . . And the glory of the Lord shall be revealed, and all flesh shall see it together: for the mouth of the Lord hath spoken it (*Isa.* 40:3, 5).

But dealing with sin is not an easy matter. None of us finds it easy to say those three little words: 'I was wrong.' Marriages frequently sputter and die because those words stick in our throats. Friendships often fester with suspicion and tension because of unwillingness to say those words. Churches are often polarized and paralyzed for the lack of these words. But difficult as they are, they must be said, and said from the heart. Let us learn from Isaiah. He does not mince words. He makes a true confession and, in doing so, shows us the ingredients of genuine repentance. Note, first, how his confession—

I. Exposes Sin

In plain, unvarnished language Isaiah lays out for all to see the prevalence of sin. Sin had triumphed over them and that triumph was evident first in the general filthiness of their behaviour (v. 6).

Isaiah looks at this filthy behaviour in two ways.

First, he considers the source of it—the uncleanness of our nature. 'We are all as an unclean thing,' he says. All our sinful acts stem from this fact that we are sinners by nature. The stream is polluted because the spring is polluted.

Nothing causes modern man to get his hackles up quicker than this kind of talk. We are fond of talking about man's basic goodness. If man fails, it is not to be construed as sinful nature exerting itself; it is simply some deficiency in his education or environment. And man's greatest need, therefore, is not salvation from sin, but improved schools and a better society.

In fact, the teaching of sinful human nature is widely considered to be positively harmful to man. It causes him

34

to have a low self-esteem. Some have gone so far as to suggest that the only salvation man needs is not from sin but from low self-esteem.

Meanwhile man goes on sinning with abandon and he continues to reap the havoc and ruin sin has to offer. While he talks glowingly about his dignity and his potential, his society crumbles all around him.

Christians have been forgiven of their sins, but the sinful nature they were born with has not been obliterated. It still exerts a powerful influence and the Christian finds it necessary constantly to cry out with the apostle Paul: 'O wretched man that I am!' (*Rom.* 7:24).

From this consideration, Isaiah turns to the scope of our filth. It extends even to our best performances. Isaiah says: 'All our righteousnesses are as filthy rags.' This statement caused Charles Spurgeon to remark: 'Brethren, if our righteousnesses are so bad, what must our unrighteousnesses be?'

So deeply ingrained is our sinfulness that it touches and taints everything we do. Theologians used to talk a good deal about man's 'total depravity.' They did not mean that man is as bad as he can be, but rather that his sinful nature shows itself in everything he does. To quote Spurgeon again:

> . . . there is sin in our very holiness, there is unbelief in our faith; there is hatred in our very love; there is the slime of the serpent upon the fairest flower of our garden.

Appalling as this description is, it is only half of the story. The other half is set forth by Isaiah in these provocative words: 'And there is none that calleth upon thy name, that stirreth up himself to take hold of thee . . .' (v. 7).

So in addition to the filthiness of their behaviour, Isaiah confesses the frigidity of their hearts. Nothing was more needful than for them to take hold of God in prayer, seek his forgiveness, and plead his promises. But this requires effort. One has to stir himself up to do this kind of thing. One has to take stock of himself, get sick of the sin he has allowed in his life, and determine that he is not going to go on in this way. But this was the very thing Isaiah's generation was not prepared to do. They were in such a state of slumber that they could not rouse themselves.

The commentator Albert Barnes puts it like this:

> No man rises to God without effort; and unless men make an effort for this, they fall into the stupidity of sin, just as certainly as a drowsy man sinks back into deep sleep.

These people, then, were caught in Satan's deadly pincers. On one side, they were involved in all kinds of filthiness. On the other side they were cold toward the Lord. Sins of commission on one hand, sins of omission on the other! Doing evil and failing to do good! What a fatal combination! And it is a combination that is being repeated innumerable times in the lives of God's people today. True repentance will not dodge either side of this combination. It will frankly expose both, and refuse to excuse either.

But there is another important aspect of true repentance illustrated by Isaiah's confession. Notice how he also—

II. Exonerates God

Because of the prevalence of sin in his nation Isaiah could also see and confess the presence of judgment. 'Thou art wroth,' says Isaiah (v.5). Yes, he actually attributes anger to God. This always leaves some dumbfounded and aghast. God angry? Yes! Time and time again the Bible tells us that God has a settled opposition to sin, and yet we refuse to believe it. We have become so infatuated with the love of God that we have forgotten about the holiness that requires him to judge sin. We are as foolish as the ostrich who, by burying his head in the sand, thinks he has escaped the hunters. You might say: 'I prefer to think of God as a God of love.' I am sure you do. But that is the 'ostrich syndrome' if ever there was one. Preferring to have only a God of love in no way negates that he is also a God who has sworn to judge sin.

From his flat affirmation of God's anger, Isaiah proceeds to employ two metaphors to convey God's judgment upon his people. One is the wind (v. 6), the other is fire (v. 7).

When God's people get involved in sin and grow cold toward the Lord, they begin to 'fade as a leaf.' Their spiritual strength begins to wither and then they are carried

37

away by the wind of judgment. The wind of God's judgment carried Isaiah's people all the way to Babylon! Such was the outcome of their ungodly living. They became 'Exhibit A' of the truth of the Psalmist's words. The man who delights in the law of the Lord is one whose 'leaf also shall not wither' (*Psa.* 1:3). But the ungodly are 'like the chaff which the wind driveth away' (*Psa.* 1:4).

Then Isaiah uses the image of fire. He says God has 'consumed us, because of our iniquities.' Fire is a common biblical symbol for judgment. It reflects the pain and anguish that comes from judgment. But the fire of judgment also carries an element of hope. It is fire that refines gold by melting away the impurities. If we are God's people, God's consuming fire will ultimately be the means of our renewal.

The thing I want you to see here is that in making this affirmation about God's anger and in using these metaphors, Isaiah does not argue with God. He simply acknowledges that God is angry, but he does not accuse God of being unfair. He does not dispute God's right to be angry over their sins. Here we come to the heart of true repentance. True repentance always honours God; it acknowledges him to be God and acknowledges his rights as God. In other words, repentance is where one stops filling his mouth with arguments against God, and takes his place as the creature before the Creator.

You will never know repentance and the peace and joy it brings as long as you are interested in defending yourself against God. 'That is not fair!' 'But I do not see how

God can do that.' These are the stock sentiments of the person who is a stranger to repentance. The one who uses them only reflects his ignorance of this statement:

> For my thoughts are not your thoughts, neither are your ways my ways, saith the LORD. For as the heavens are higher than the earth, so are my ways higher than your ways, and my thoughts than your thoughts (*Isa.* 55:8, 9).

Here then in Isaiah's prayer is ground we must occupy if we truly desire the Lord to 'Come down'. We must repent of our sins. We must not gloss over them, but frankly acknowledge them. And we must recognize God's judgment is right and just. Let our prayer today be: 'Come down, Lord, we have wronged you!'

QUESTIONS FOR DISCUSSION

1. What is repentance?

2. Why do think there is so little talk about repentance in the church today?

3. What does the author identify in this chapter as 'deadly pincers?'

4. What does fire often symbolize in the Bible?

39

6

WE BELONG TO YOU

But now, O Lord, *thou art our father; we are the clay, and thou our potter: and we all are the work of thy hand.*

Be not wroth very sore, O Lord, *neither remember iniquity for ever; behold, see, we beseech thee, we are all thy people.*

The holy cities are a wilderness, Zion is a wilderness, Jerusalem a desolation.

Our holy and our beautiful house, where our fathers praised thee, is burned up with fire: and all our pleasant things are laid waste.

Wilt thou refrain thyself for these things, O Lord? *wilt thou hold thy peace, and afflict us very sore?* (Isaiah 64:8-12)

We have been following the prophet Isaiah as he pleads with God to come down in renewing, revitalizing power. Isaiah has used several powerful arguments, but here he pulls out all the stops. He holds before God the fact of his covenant with them. In essence, Isaiah is saying God has to come down and renew his people because they are his people. 'We all are the work of thy hand,' cries Isaiah (v. 8). And a little later he adds: 'We are all thy people' (v. 9). He even goes so far as to call the cities of Judah God's cities (v. 10).

In arguing this way, Isaiah is following in the steps of another great man of God, Moses. On more than one occasion Moses pleaded with God not to destroy the people of Israel because of the covenant God had made with them. Moses' argument was if God destroyed the people, the enemies of God would ridicule God by saying he was not able to take Israel into the promised land. God had promised to do this, and Moses held before him that promise. In effect, Moses was saying to God: 'If you destroy these people, you will lose more than they will, because your honour is at stake here. You must do as you have promised' (see *Exod.* 32:9-14, *Num.* 14:11-20).

There is, then, a daring quality to Isaiah's prayer. Isaiah is reminding God that he has obligated himself to his people, that his honour is at stake. This is true praying, and the fact that we hear so little of it today is an indication of how low we are spiritually. If we are to begin praying in this bold and daring way, we must understand the implications of belonging to God. If we truly belong to God, we must confess first—

I. God Has Been Good To Us

How long has it been since you really savoured this— the privilege of being a child of God? Consider God for a moment. Isaiah consistently refers to him as 'LORD' in this prayer (63:16-17; 64:8-9, 12). And what is it to be 'LORD'? It is to be absolutely sovereign. This is God according to Isaiah. He is the absolute, sovereign ruler of everything.

The way Isaiah begins this prayer tells us much about God. Isaiah says: 'Look down from heaven . . . ' (63:15). God is so highly exalted, he has to look down. He far surpasses and transcends all of us. Then Isaiah adds: 'behold from the habitation of thy holiness and thy glory . . .'. There is the greatness of God! His habitation is holy and glorious. Holiness and glory surround him all the time.

Later in this prayer, Isaiah says God is so great that he is beyond our ability to comprehend or describe:

> . . . men have not heard, nor perceived by the ear, neither hath the eye seen, O God, beside thee, what he hath prepared for him that waiteth for him. (64:4)

We will never fully appreciate what it means to belong to God if we do not begin here. Begin with the majesty and glory of God, and you will appreciate the marvel of Isaiah saying: 'Thou, O LORD, art our Father . . .' (63:16; 64:8). How astonishing! Here is this incomparable, incomprehensible God who sovereignly rules over all, and yet we call him Father! How can such a thing be? There is only one answer—this God has stooped down in grace to us and made it possible for us to know him. If we belong to God, it is no credit to us. There was nothing in us to commend us to God. God had to reach down to us.

Do you appreciate what it is to belong to this God? As the supreme ruler of this universe, he could simply snuff us out with one word. But he has chosen to make his children those who trust him. Oh, what a privilege it is to belong to God! How good he has been to those who know him!

The next thing that belonging to God implies is—

II. We Should Honour God

After all he has done for us, this should be our natural response. But I am afraid we are no kinder to God than Isaiah's people. Isaiah surveys his people and he is compelled to confess that they have not lived up to their privileges. In fact, Isaiah's whole prayer is a scathing, scalding indictment upon his people.

So badly had his people treated God that Isaiah says several things. First, they would be unrecognized by their fathers (63:16). Isaiah says if Jacob could look at them, he would not even acknowledge them as his descendants. So completely had they departed from their heritage, they would not even be claimed by the originators of their heritage.

Further, Isaiah says his people were utterly unimpressive to their foes (63:18). They were completely trodden down by their enemies. There was nothing about them as the people of God that would strike the smallest tremor in the hearts of their enemies.

Beyond that, Isaiah concludes that they were undistinguished from their fellows (63:19). The people of God had become like those over whom God had never ruled (such is the translation of the New

King James Version and the New American Standard Bible). In other words, the people of God in Isaiah's day looked exactly like the pagans all around them. There was nothing different or distinctive about God's own people.

If we want to know whether we are appreciating our privileges and living as the people of God should, we can use Isaiah's descriptions of his people as questions to test ourselves. Are we living in such a way that those who have been faithful in the past would be glad to claim us as their descendants? Or have we departed from our heritage? Are those who are opposed to Christianity aware that there is something special about us? Do they feel any awe as they look at us or do they just snicker at us? Is there anything that sets us apart from the unbelieving multitudes all around us, or do we just blend in with the paganism of our day?

It seems to me that we only have to raise these questions in order to have our answer. We really are not treating God any better than Isaiah's people. And because of that we sorely need to hear the third implication of belonging to God. It is that—

III. God Can Do With Us As He Pleases

We do not much like to hear about this, but it is a natural inference of belonging to God. If we are his and we have not been treating him as we should, we can expect him to do with us as he did with Isaiah's people—chastise!

Chastisement is never a pleasant thing, but it is always profitable. Isaiah's people had sinned against the Lord in incalculable ways. They had scorned their heritage and chased unashamedly after other gods. They had abandoned themselves to all kinds of immorality and promiscuity. So what did God do? Did he simply pace around heaven, fretting about what to do and wringing his hands? Do not believe it for a second! God is never at a loss as to how to handle sin in the lives of his people. He patiently endured their sin for several years and sent men like Isaiah to warn them and call them to repentance. But when they stubbornly persisted in their rebellion, God brought the Babylonians upon them and they were carried off into captivity. There they spent seventy years reflecting upon their folly, and only then were they moved to pray this prayer that Isaiah knew they would be praying. God finally heard their prayer and restored them to their land.

Do you object to God handling his people in this way? Be careful, my friend, about what you say. Remember he is God and it is not for man to reply against God (*Rom.* 9:20), and remember that as his people they belonged to him and he could do with them as he pleased. Remember also that God has not changed one iota, and he will bring chastisement upon his people today if they persist in disobedience.

But I must not leave it there. There is one more implication of belonging to God, and it is—

45

IV. God Will Never Disown Us

Chastisement is never God's final word. No one can put it better than the psalmist: 'For his anger endureth but a moment; in his favour is life: weeping may endure for a moment, but joy cometh in the morning' (*Psa.* 30:5).

The best thing about belonging to God is that no matter how far away we stray, we can, like the prodigal son in Jesus' parable, always go home. Isaiah knew this, so he closed his prayer with these words: 'Wilt thou refrain thyself for these things, O LORD? wilt thou hold thy peace, and afflict us very sore?' (64:12). In those questions there is the implicit faith that God cannot let his people go on in the misery and pain of chastisement, that he was waiting anxiously to restore them.

Let God himself explain why we do not have to worry about him disowning us:

> Can a woman forget her sucking child, that she should not have compassion on the son of her womb? yea, they may forget, yet will I not forget thee. Behold, I have graven thee upon the palms of my hands; thy walls are continually before me (*Isa.* 49:15, 16).

Fortified with such words, why do we continue to muddle along in our spiritual deadness and barrenness? Why do we not remind God of his promises and expectantly look forward to his blessings? Why not chime in with Isaiah: 'Come down, Lord; we belong to you!'

QUESTIONS FOR DISCUSSION

1. Identify some of the ways in which God has been good to you. What is the supreme expression of his goodness to you?

2. What does it mean to honour God?

3. What does Isaiah identify as the result of God's people refusing to honour God?

4. What does chastisement mean? Why does God chastise his people?

5. What do you consider to be the ultimate proof that God will not disown his people?

7

WE BESEECH YOU

Be not wroth very sore, O Lord, neither remember iniquity for ever: behold, see, we beseech thee, we are all thy people (Isaiah 64:9).

It appears that many Christians have just about given up on prayer. They retain it as a form to keep appearances up, but secretly they regard it as an exercise in futility. They harbour suspicions that God is so reluctant and miserly he will not grant their requests; or worse yet, he does not even hear prayer in the first place.

But the Bible insists the problem is not with God. It consistently pictures God as anxious and eager to bless. The psalmist says:

> The Lord is nigh unto all them that call upon him, to all that call upon him in truth. He will fulfill the desire of them that fear him: he will also hear their cry, and save them (*Psa.*145:18, 19).

If the problem is not with God, then there must be something wrong with our prayers. Did you notice the condition the psalmist attached to the Lord being nigh? He is nigh to all that 'call upon him in truth.' Ah, there is the rub! We want to toss up casual, lukewarm petitions, and then we get peeved when God does not come through for us.

If we want the Lord to hear and answer prayer, we must realize that even though he is favourably disposed to the prayers of his people, he does not count everything we call prayer as prayer. In other words, we need to learn to pray.

Isaiah really models true praying for us. He summarizes what prayer is all about in those three little words: 'We beseech thee.' Let us delve into those words and seek to understand what they convey. First, there is quite obviously an—

I. Intensity of Desire

The word 'beseech' is a strong word. It is much stronger than 'ask' or 'request.' Those words are mild. 'Beseech' is fervent and feverish with passion. There is grime on the hands and sweat on the brow of this word. It means to entreat, to implore, to beg, to plead. There is no easy-going moderation in 'beseech.'

Isaiah has already indicated something of the nature of prayer. He has called it a stirring up of one's self to 'take hold' of God. Prayer is more than just a polite antiseptic asking of God to 'bless', it is taking hold of God. What is it to take hold of God? It is to plead God's promises before him and to refuse to take no for an answer. There is more to come on that, but for now please note that one cannot take hold of God without an intense longing for God.

Look through the Bible and you will find that the people who really did business with God were those who knew an intense longing for God. Check out the accounts of Hannah (*1 Sam.* 1:9-18), Nehemiah (*Neh.* 1:4-11), and the great Moses (*Exod.*33:12-23).

Here is how the psalmist described his longing for God: 'As the hart panteth after the water brooks, so panteth my soul after thee, O God. My soul thirsteth for God, for the living God . . .' (*Psa.* 42:1-2). Later we find him saying: '. . . my heart and my flesh cry out for the living God' (*Psa.* 84:2).

Do we really need to look any further for the explanation for unanswered prayer? How many of us really know this intensity of desire? We have been looking at the theme of revival. That is what Isaiah was praying for. But why is it so rare to see a genuine spiritual awakening among God's people? Could it not be that most of us, despite our protestations, do not really want a mighty work of God? Is it not true that genuine revival would mess up the way we are living and make us extremely uncomfortable?

For years now we have proceeded on the basis that God's people want revival and all that remains is for us to figure out how to have one. Is it not time to face up to the fact that we have been assuming the wrong thing? It seems to me that we Christians need to get our 'wanters' fixed. We want God to do a great thing but we do not want it intensely enough to earnestly seek it, or to run the risk of having our lives disturbed.

Where does intense desire for revival come from? It can come only as we look around and take note of the needs. This is what created strong desire in Isaiah. He looked at his nation and saw what she was doing and also what she was facing, and his heart was moved. I find myself wondering how bad things will have to get in our society before God's people get alarmed. The abortion industry continues its booming business. Pornography is churned out in massive doses. Homes are falling apart at a record pace. Christianity is openly disdained and ridiculed. How much more do we have to see before we get burdened? When we turn our critical gaze on the professing church in our own time, our sense of shame and alarm should increase. We ourselves are too often moulded by the patterns of thought and of life-style around us. We need to remember Christ's words to the churches, 'I know your works', and realise that if we abuse his grace he will come to us in judgment. We will never be burdened for our society while we are secretly enjoying the sinful life-style it promotes!

But there is a second element in true praying which we must examine.

II. Humility of Heart

'We beseech thee,' says Isaiah. Anyone who is in the position of beseeching is one who cannot help himself. He is powerless. He is completely dependent upon someone else to come to his aid or he would not be beseeching. In other words, humility is part and parcel of this business of beseeching God.

Humility is woven into the whole fabric of Isaiah's prayer. The very fact that God is in heaven and has to 'look down' (63:15), tells us that Isaiah is conscious of God's greatness and man's unworthiness. In confessing the filthiness of their sins (64:5-7), Isaiah was putting himself and his people in the dust before God.

You can take this to the bank—true praying is humble praying. The Bible says: 'He forgetteth not the cry of the humble' (*Psa.* 9:12). And again: 'Though the Lord be high, yet hath he respect unto the lowly' (*Psa.* 138:6).

And while you are going to the bank, take this along too—revival comes only to the humble. The best known verse on revival begins: 'If my people, who are called by my name, shall humble themselves, and pray' (2 *Chron.* 7:14).

One of the more worrisome features of our day is the cloaking of arrogance in spirituality. We seem to regard arrogance as a trademark of being close to God. Some have grown very fond of talking about what 'the Lord is doing in my life,' and somehow the 'my life' always sounds louder than 'the Lord.' It is also common today to hear people pray: 'Thank you Lord for what you are showing me in my quiet time.' Is it not enough just to thank the Lord for his Word? Do we have to advertise ourselves and the spiritual disciplines we seek to maintain? If our 'quiet time' is nothing more than a badge of our supposed superior spirituality, we are no better than the pious Pharisees of Jesus' day! How we need to heed the words of Andrew Murray: 'The chief mark of counterfeit holiness is its lack of humility.'

The only remedy for pride is to dwell much on the holiness and majesty of God. It was when Isaiah saw the Lord 'high and lifted up' that he cried out,

> Woe is me! For I am undone, because I am a man of unclean lips, and I dwell in the midst of a people of unclean lips; for mine eyes have seen the King, the LORD of hosts (*Isa.* 6:5).

That brings us to the third element of true praying—

III. Tenacity of Purpose

This is closely related to the intensity of desire. If we are truly longing for God to answer prayer, if we are truly beseeching God, we will not give up easily. True praying is persistent praying.

Jesus emphasized on more than one occasion the need for being tenacious in prayer. Luke recalls one parable that was designed to teach 'that men ought always to pray, and not to faint' (*Luke* 18:1). It had to do with a woman who kept pestering a judge. This woman had some legal problem that she wanted the judge to take care of for her. The problem was this judge was notorious for being unconcerned about people and their needs. This woman did not let that deter her. She went to the judge and cried out 'avenge me of mine adversary.' The judge refused. But the woman did not let it rest there. She continued to pester the judge. We might picture her being at his office each day, following him through the streets to his home, and staying outside his home. Every time he turned around, there she was. Finally, in order to be free of her, he granted her request (*Luke* 18:1-8).

God is not like that unjust judge. God is concerned about the needs of His people. And if a judge like that can be persuaded by persistence, how much more reason we have to expect God to reward our persistence in prayer!

But some will ask why it is necessary for us to be persistent in prayer. After all, if God knows we need something, why does he not just give it to us? The answer is that we need to be persistent not so much for God's sake as for ours. Benefits easily gained are not duly prized. That which has been won by toil and hardship will be guarded diligently, while that which comes to us easily will be squandered carelessly away.

In other words, by being persistent in prayer we show how highly we prize God's blessings, and God is more inclined to grant his blessings to those who prize them. Isaiah had determined that he and his people so desperately needed God that he would not rest until God renewed them (*Isa.* 62:1,6-7). When we decide we cannot live without God, we shall become as tenacious in prayer as Isaiah was.

In light of these things, is it not time we stopped blaming God for unanswered prayer and began looking to ourselves? How many of us pray, halfheartedly, selfishly, and spasmodically? Is it not time we stopped muddling along without God's power and began to pray with intensity, humility, and tenacity? May God help us to begin today.

QUESTIONS FOR DISCUSSION

1. Why do God's people sometimes give up on prayer?

2. How does the author define the word 'beseech?'

3. What is necessary to have an intense desire for revival?

4. What does the author identify as the remedy for pride?

5. Why do you think God wants his people to be persistent in prayer?

EPILOGUE

These pages have been written with the dual conviction that God is hiding his face from his people, and that it is not an easy thing to seek his face.

The church today seems largely unwilling to face either of these realities.

She insists on one hand that God really is blessing her, and to prove it she cites all kinds of glowing statistics. But statistics can never measure the spiritual climate of the church. The church can have impressive statistics and be sorely lacking in holiness and spiritual power. Sadly, the church has often used statistics to pull the wool over her own eyes. A church can be bustling with activity and bursting at the seams and at the same time be infiltrated and permeated with the world's thinking and doing.

True revival cannot come as long as the church insists she is all right.

Then there is the other problem. Sometimes the church does catch a glimpse of her desperate condition. But what is her response? All too often it has been to think that revival can come easily and quickly. We seek revival too casually and claim it too rapidly. Repentance is painstaking work. Glossing over it will never bring an extraordinary work of God.

Isaiah's prayer gives full play to each of these. His prayer 'Come down, Lord!' reflects his understanding of God's distance and of the need for thorough repentance. My hope is that all those who read this will catch Isaiah's vision and join in his prayer.